DATE DUE

JAPAN
IN THE DAYS OF
THE SAMURAI

To Joyce Stanton,
editor, inspiration, and friend

⁓

With thanks to Yasuko Makino, Japanese Studies Librarian,
Columbia University, New York City,
for her thoughtful reading of the manuscript

The poems on page 26–27 and the haiku beginning "Spring soon ends" and "A village" on page 27 are reprinted from *Anthology of Japanese Literature* by Donald Keene. The haiku beginning "This ancient pond" is reprinted from *In the Shogun's Shadow* by John Langone. "Summer grasses" is from *Samurai: The Story of a Warrior Tradition* by Harry Cook.

CULTURES
OF THE PAST

JAPAN
IN THE DAYS OF
THE SAMURAI

VIRGINIA SCHOMP

BENCHMARK BOOKS

MARSHALL CAVENDISH

NEW YORK

Benchmark Books
Marshall Cavendish Corporation
99 White Plains Road
Tarrytown, New York 10591-9001

Website: www.marshallcavendish.com

© Marshall Cavendish Corporation 2002

Library of Congress Cataloging-in-Publication Data
Schomp, Virginia.
    Japan in the days of the samurai / Virginia Schomp.
       p.   cm.— (Cultures of the past)
    Includes bibliographical references and index.
    Summary: Describes the Japanese way of life during the samurai eras through information about the politics, military, culture, and the belief system; also indicates the legacy of the period.
    ISBN 0-7614-0304-3
    1. Japan—Civilization—To 1868—Juvenile literature. [1. Japan—Civilization—To 1868.] I. Title. II. Series.
DS822.2.S35   2001
952—dc21
                                                      98-12228

Printed in Hong Kong

1 3 5 6 4 2

Book design by Carol Matsuyama
Photo research by Rose Corbett Gordon

Front cover: A Kabuki actor plays the role of a samurai in this nineteenth-century wood-block print.

Back cover: A nineteenth-century wood-block print of a scene from *The Tale of Genji*, the world's first novel

Photo Credits
Front cover: courtesy of Werner Forman/Art Resource, NY; back cover: courtesy of Private Collection/Bridgeman Art Library; pages 6–7, 15, 40, 67: Werner Forman/Art Resource, NY; page 6: Earth Imaging/Stone Images; page 9: Victoria & Albert Museum, London, UK/Bridgeman Art Library; pages 11, 45: Laurie Platt Winfrey/Bradley Smith Collection; page 13: The Art Archive/Victoria and Albert Museum, London/Eileen Tweedy; page 17: Werner Forman Archive/HM DeYoung Memorial Museum, San Francisco, USA; page 20: The Metropolitan Museum of Art, Purchase, Joseph Pulitzer, Bequest, 1918, (JP 601); page 21: The British Museum, London, UK/Bridgeman Art Library; pages 24–25: Fitzwilliam Museum, University of Cambridge, UK/Bridgeman Art Library; page 26: David Bull Collection; pages 28–19: Private Collection/Bridgeman Art Library; page 30: Giraudon/Art Resource, NY; page 31: Bonhams, London, UK/Bridgeman Art Library; page 32: Private Collection/Bridgeman Art Library; pages 34–35: Christie's Images/Bridgeman Art Library; page 36: Japan National Tourist Office; page 37: Wrangham Collection/Bridgeman Art Library; page 39: Demetrio Carrasco/Stone Images; page 42: © Bigelow Collection, courtesy of Museum of Fine Arts, Boston; page 43: Stone Images; page 47: Paul Chesley/Stone Images; pages 50–51: Victoria & Albert Museum, London/Art Resource, NY; page 54: © David Ball/The Picture Cube, Inc.; page 55: Ryoko-in Daitoku-ji, Kyoto; page 58: Japan Archives; page 61: Hulton Getty/Liaison Agency; page 63: Charles Gupton/Stone Images; page 66: © T. Chinami/The Image Bank; page 68: Thierry Cazabon/Stone Images

CONTENTS

CHAPTER ONE

LIVING GODS AND WARRIORS

Some one hundred miles off the east coast of Asia lies the island nation called Japan. For most of its history this chain of green islands was a mystery to the outside world. Surrounded by rough seas, Japan was largely cut off from other peoples and places. During centuries of almost complete isolation the Japanese invented their own unique and fascinating culture.

Isolation was just one of the geographical facts that shaped the growth of Japan. To understand the other key fact, we must look at the land itself. Mountains and wooded hills cover four-fifths of Japan. The country's history is the story of conflict over the remaining fifth. For centuries landowners fought to protect their precious patches of flat, fertile farmland and to capture new lands from their neighbors. A complex system of government grew out of these struggles. At the heart of that system was the class of warriors known as samurai (SA-muh-rye).

Japan is made up of more than four thousand islands strung out like a necklace off the eastern coast of Asia.

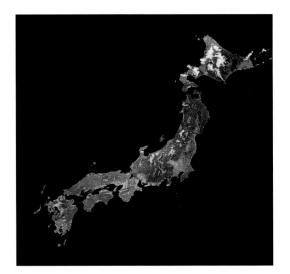

Loyal servants, cruel assassins, poets, avengers, peacekeepers—the samurai played many roles. For nearly a thousand years they were the most powerful force in Japanese government and society. To many people the samurai remain a shining example of the unique Japanese spirit.

Fierce warriors and master swordsmen, the samurai dominated Japanese government and society for centuries.

Divine Rulers

The roots of the samurai reach deep into Japan's past. Two thousand years ago the Japanese lived in clans, or large groups of related families. These clans battled one another for land and power. They buried their chiefs in earthen mounds more massive than the pyramids of Egypt. Among the treasures placed in their burial mounds were small statues of sword-wielding warriors.

By 400 C.E.* the Yamato clan had won control over most of the country. The Yamato claimed that their leaders were descended from Japan's most important sacred being, the sun goddess Amaterasu. That made the Yamato emperors and empresses the country's natural rulers. Other clans did not dare attack the "living gods" who sat on the throne. Instead the strongest families found ways to control the imperial family and so to control Japan.

In 593 the leader of the Soga clan made his nephew, Prince Shotoku, regent to the Yamato empress. As chief adviser to the country's ruler, the regent was the most powerful figure in Japan. Shotoku sent ambassadors to neighboring China, home of the world's most advanced civilization. He used ideas borrowed from the Chinese to transform Japan's government, science, religion, and arts.

After Shotoku's death the Fujiwara clan rose to power. Under the leadership of Fujiwara regents, Japan continued its transformation. A new culture emerged, combining foreign and native ideas in a blend that was uniquely Japanese. Some of the greatest changes came in government: Japan's leaders, to increase their control of the country, declared that all land belonged to the emperor. Important clan members became nobles in the imperial court, governing their former lands in the emperor's name.

Birth of the Samurai

In 794 the emperor and the Fujiwara leaders founded a new capital in Heian, later called Kyoto. Here elegantly dressed nobles spent their days gossiping, playing music, and composing poetry.

The luxuries of Kyoto court life were paid for by taxes collected

*Many systems of dating have been used by different cultures throughout history. This series of books uses B.C.E. (Before Common Era) and C.E. (Common Era) instead of B.C. (Before Christ) and A.D. (Anno Domini) out of respect for the diversity of the world's peoples.

from the people who managed and worked the emperor's lands. But powerful clan leaders, bending the laws in their own favor, began to take over those lands. Between the ninth and twelfth centuries they carved up the countryside. Once again Japan became a patchwork of private estates.

Hundreds of nobles waited on Japan's revered emperors amid the luxuries of the imperial court.

As the estate owners grew rich and strong, the Fujiwara government became poor and weak. Government forces could no longer keep order. Bandits roamed the countryside, and pirates ruled the seas. To protect their estates, wealthy landowners began raising their own private armies of soldiers, who promised unquestioning loyalty and service. These proud, skillful warriors called themselves "those who serve," or samurai.

The Gempei War

By the early twelfth century samurai armies had become the most powerful fighting forces in Japan. The fiercest warriors served the Taira and Minamoto clans. The armies of these clans were so respected that the emperor and the Fujiwara court nobles began using them to settle their own fights. As the samurai took sides in battles over the country's leadership, they began to realize how weak the central government had become.

Around 1160 the Taira swept the Fujiwara from power. Then the Minamoto tried to overthrow the Taira. The rivalry between the two clans led to a six-year civil war known as the Gempei War.

The final battle of the Gempei War took place at sea in 1185. The Taira forces had suffered one defeat after another. Now their four hundred ships faced a much larger Minamoto fleet near a beach called Dan-no-ura. Sailing on one of the Taira warships was the emperor, eight-year-old Antoku.

The Tale of the Heike, a thirteenth-century collection of stories, describes how the Taira forces faced defeat. Antoku's grandmother "took the Emperor in her arms and said, 'Though I am but a woman, I will not fall into the hands of the enemy. . . . In the depths of the ocean is our capital.'" The old woman told Antoku to say his prayers. Then, holding the boy tightly, she stepped off the ship and "sank with him at last beneath the waves." Following their example, thousands of Taira soldiers and court ladies leaped into the sea and drowned.

After the Minamoto victory a new emperor took the throne in Kyoto, but he was more than ever a powerless puppet. The real power belonged to Minamoto Yoritomo,* leader of the victorious clan. Yoritomo made the emperor grant him the title "barbarian-subduing general," or shogun. He settled in the eastern seaside town of Kamakura. There he established a

---

*In Japan, the family name comes first, followed by the given name. After the full name is mentioned once, only the given name is used.

new type of government based on the courage and loyalty of the samurai.

Mongol Invasions

"Duty . . . is the making of a samurai," says a thirteenth-century book of advice written by a Japanese father for his samurai son. Duty and loyalty were the forces that held together the shogunate, the military government established by Yoritomo. The all-powerful shogun appointed high-ranking samurai to serve as his stewards and governors. Bound by an oath of loyalty, these samurai lords governed Japan's villages and private estates, kept the peace, and collected the taxes.

Each samurai lord had his own army of warriors, who swore complete loyalty to him. Poems and novels celebrated the courage and fighting skills of these warriors. Samurai trained constantly to perfect their mastery of sword and bow. They rushed into the fiercest battles, eager for glory. Above all they lived by a code of honor that came to be called Bushido (BU-shee-doh), or "the way of the warrior."

In the late thirteenth century the samurai's fighting skills faced their greatest test. The Mongols, fierce conquerors from northern Asia, had already overrun China, Korea, and most of eastern Europe. In 1274 their leader, Kublai Khan, turned his ferocious forces toward Japan. The samurai were nearly defeated in a brief, desperate battle on the shores of Kyushu Island. Then the invaders were forced to call off their attack when a violent storm destroyed most of their fleet.

Seven years later the Mongols struck again. More than 140,000 soldiers attacked Kyushu's northern coast. Heroic samurai defenders held off the invaders during two months of furious fighting. Japan was saved once again by a sudden raging storm, which pounded the Mongols' ships to pieces. Joyously the Japanese

In 1192 samurai chief Minamoto Yoritomo became Japan's first shogun, or military ruler.

Samurai warriors lived by Bushido, a code of behavior that covered nearly every area of life. Bushido demanded that a samurai show absolute loyalty and obedience to his lord. He must gladly face danger, even death, in the performance of his duties. The *Hagakure*, an eighteenth-century collection of writings on Bushido, proclaims, "The way of the Samurai is death. . . . When a samurai is constantly prepared for death, he . . . may unerringly devote his life to the service of his lord."

The samurai who failed his lord suffered a dishonor worse than death. There was only one way to erase the disgrace. The samurai must commit seppuku (seh-POO-koo), sometimes called hara-kiri (hair-ih-KIR-ee), or "belly slitting." In this horribly painful form of suicide, the dishonored samurai used a short sword to cut open his belly and release his spirit.

Bushido demanded that samurai live pure, simple lives. They must show dignity, respect, and quiet confidence. The ideal samurai knew the proper way to walk, bow, hold his chopsticks, remove enemy heads in battle, and display them afterward. He knew the value of honesty. "Never say a single word of falsehood or even half of it," samurai warlord Hojo Soun counseled in the 1400s. Soun also advised his samurai followers to study poetry, reading, and writing. "Hold literary skills in your left hand," he wrote, "martial [warlike] skills in your right. This is the law from ancient times."

gave thanks to the kamikaze (kah-mih-KAH-zee), the "divine wind" sent to save the gods' favored islands.

Two Warring Courts

After the Mongol invasions the samurai who had defended Japan expected rich rewards from their leaders in Kamakura. But the Hojo, the family that now controlled the shogunate, had little land or treasure to give. The samurai felt betrayed. Some wanted the Hojo replaced by a strong new shogun. Others believed it was time for the emperor to gain real power.

In 1333 samurai supporters of Emperor Go-Daigo marched to Kamakura and wiped out the Hojo forces. Then an ambitious samurai general, Ashikaga Takauji, turned against Go-Daigo. Takauji forced the emperor out of Kyoto and placed another member of the imperial family on the throne. Suddenly Japan had *two* emperors: Go-Daigo, called the Emperor of the South, and Takauji's puppet emperor, the Emperor of the North.

For nearly sixty years war raged between supporters of the two courts. First one group and then the other gained the upper hand. At last the northern forces proved strongest. In 1392 Japan was reunited under a single emperor, controlled by an Ashikaga shogun.

The Country at War

Ashikaga shoguns governed Japan for the next two centuries. Under their rule the arts flourished and the economy prospered through trade with China. But the Ashikaga were not strong enough to control all of the country. The wealthy landowners they appointed to govern the countryside fought among themselves for property and power. Kyoto, the Ashikaga capital, was the governors' main battleground. After their worst conflict, the ten-year Onin War, much of that beautiful city lay in ruins.

The Onin War marked the beginning of the Age of the Country at War, from 1467 to 1568. During that century of struggle the large

Shogun Ashikaga Takauji holds court in his capital at Kyoto. During Ashikaga rule, Japan was torn by constant warfare.

landowners completely wiped one another out. The shogun's authority faded to nothing. Constant fighting and peasant riots tore apart Japan's villages and cities.

In the midst of this chaos small samurai landowners began to build their own armies. Many of their soldiers were farmers who turned over their lands in return for protection and favor. Over time these new warlords used their growing armies to build large private domains. Japan became a nation of independent states, each ruled by an all-powerful warlord, or daimyo (DIE-mee-oh).

Japan's Feudal System

The daimyo were like kings in their private domains. They lived in castles surrounded by the towns and farming villages of their kingdoms. Everyone residing in a daimyo's territory—those who turned over their lands willingly as well as those whose lands were conquered—swore an oath of loyalty to the lord and promised to serve him in times of war. In return the daimyo gave his vassals, or followers, land and a guarantee of protection. This type of political system, based on bonds of loyalty between lord and vassal, is known as feudalism. The feudal system had been developing in Japan since the earliest days of the samurai. Now, under the powerful and independent daimyo, it reached its full growth.

Feudalism brought the first real improvements to the lives of Japan's peasant farmers. Since ancient times peasants had toiled like slaves on their small patches of land. Often they had been forced to turn over most of the rice they grew to government officials. Under the daimyo they were allowed to keep a larger portion of their crops. Some peasant vassals rose from poverty to become merchants, who made their living through trade, or artisans, who crafted goods such as cloth, swords, and armor. Some peasants joined their lord's army. These lower-class foot soldiers were called *ashigaru* (ahsh-ee-gah-roo), or "light feet." Armed with spears and blade-tipped poles, *ashigaru* troops made well-ordered, effective fighting forces.

The heart of the armies, though, was still the samurai. Constant warfare gave these honored soldiers plenty of chances to prove their worth. Some samurai became master swordsmen and started martial arts schools to teach their secret skills. Some served their daimyo as spies, collecting information in enemy domains.

The most deadly spies were the ninja, experts in the "art of invisibility." Dressed in black and acting under cover of darkness, a ninja might slip past a castle's guards to steal military secrets or murder a sleeping lord. Nervous daimyo often installed "burglar alarms" to outsmart the ninja. Nijo Castle in Kyoto had a special "nightingale floor" that squeaked like a noisy bird when anyone ventured near the lord's private chambers.

A ninja spy displays the secret document he has stolen for his daimyo master.

The Path to Unity

Through war after war Japan's strongest daimyo gobbled up their neighbors' lands. By the mid–sixteenth century a handful of mighty regional rulers remained. Each warlord had a single overriding ambition: to defeat his rivals and make all Japan his domain.

A storm at sea brought new ammunition for this contest. Around 1542 high winds washed a big Chinese ship ashore in southern Japan. On board were three travelers from Portugal—the first Westerners the Japanese had ever seen. The travelers' strange clothes and manners excited much curiosity. Even more interesting were the muskets they carried. A Japanese scholar described with wonder the strange new weapon whose "explosion is like lightning and the report [noise] like thunder."

Within six months Japanese metalworkers were turning out copies of the Western muskets. The first daimyo to prove the weapons' value was Oda Nobunaga. This able young warlord rose to power through the conquest of neighboring domains. In 1575 his army faced the dreaded spear-wielding samurai of the Takeda clan. As the Takeda horsemen charged, they met a wall of bullets fired from the muskets of Nobunaga's *ashigaru* forces. More than ten thousand Takeda warriors perished. Never had a samurai battle ended with such a quick and deadly stroke.

By 1582 Nobunaga had won control of one-third of Japan. But his plans for complete conquest were cut short when he was murdered by one of his followers. To avenge Nobunaga's death, the warlord's loyal general Toyotomi Hideyoshi destroyed the traitor's forces. Then Hideyoshi took over Nobunaga's vast domain. Soon his huge, well-trained army had forced all rival lords to accept him as master. By 1590 Hideyoshi ruled a united Japan.

Eager to build an even greater empire, Hideyoshi turned his sights toward China and Korea. In 1592 he launched a huge invasion of those lands. Though the samurai won some hard-fought battles, Japan's first attempt at overseas conquest was a failure. In 1598 Hideyoshi died, and the invading forces were called home.

The Great Peace

After Hideyoshi's death there was a scramble for power. In 1600 the country's strongest warlord, Tokugawa Ieyasu, won control of Japan.

A Portuguese merchant takes a stroll beneath an umbrella held by his servant. The opening of trade with Portugal and other Western nations brought Japan new products and ideas.

Ieyasu took the old title of shogun in 1603. He set up his capital in the little fishing village of Edo.

For the next two and a half centuries Tokugawa shoguns ruled Japan. It was the longest peaceful period the country had ever known. The Tokugawa ensured order through strict government controls. About three hundred daimyo, all vassals of the shogun, ruled their domains under that leader's watchful eye. The

THREE MIGHTY SAMURAI

According to an old Japanese saying, "Nobunaga piled the rice, Hideyoshi kneaded the dough, and Tokugawa ate the cake." These three samurai were determined to build a united Japan. They succeeded through a mixture of cunning, cruelty, and brilliant leadership.

Oda Nobunaga often entertained his men with a dance and a song before battles. But this ruthless general never showed his gentler side to those he conquered. When the defenders of a mountaintop temple offered to surrender to his forces, Nobunaga built a wall around their buildings and set them on fire. Twenty thousand people were burned alive.

Toyotomi Hideyoshi was not quite as brutal to his enemies. In fact, as part of his campaign to unite Japan, Hideyoshi often forgave defeated enemies who promised to become faithful followers. One of this samurai general's most successful battle tactics was the siege. To conquer a rival daimyo, he would trap the lord and his followers in their castle. One daimyo was forced to surrender when Hideyoshi's men flooded his castle with waters from a nearby river. Another held out until the general's miners dug under his castle walls and brought them tumbling down.

Tokugawa Ieyasu sometimes used trickery to strengthen his hold on Japan. After Ieyasu became shogun, the only remaining challenger to his authority was Hideyoshi's son, Toyotomi Hideyori. In 1614 Ieyasu persuaded Hideyori to accept a truce. While the two sides talked peace, the shogun's men secretly filled in the moats around Hideyori's Osaka Castle. Then Ieyasu attacked the castle, easily overcoming its weakened defenses.

daimyo had to spend every other year at the shogun's court. When they returned to their domains, their wives and children remained in Edo. By holding their families as hostages, the shogun ensured the daimyo's loyalty through the coming year.

Other Tokugawa policies controlled marriage, housing, business, dress, behavior—every area of life. The laws drew sharp lines between the different social classes. At the bottom of the social scale were the merchants and artisans. Next came the farmers. Forced to turn over at least half of their crops to the shogun, most farmers were very poor. Laws dictated when and where these commoners could travel, what clothes they must wear each season, even what types of dolls they could give their children.

Far above the farmers on the social scale were the samurai. As members of the upper class, these "peacetime warriors" had many special privileges. Only the samurai were permitted to carry two swords. If a commoner displeased a samurai, the warrior had the right to immediately slice off the offender's head.

The samurai themselves were divided into different social levels, from the shogun and the highest-ranking daimyo all the way down to the lowest *ashigaru*. Laws prevented the samurai from working for themselves. In peace as in war their duty was to serve their lord. For low-level samurai, service might mean guarding the castles, repairing the highways, or policing the streets. Higher-ranking samurai usually tended to their daimyo's business affairs.

The only person above the shogun in social ranking was the emperor. The Tokugawa shoguns were careful to pay their respects to the imperial court, issuing all government orders in the sacred emperor's name. As always, though, the emperor had no real political power. Like a prisoner in a golden cage, Japan's divine ruler lived an elegant life at court, watched over by the shogun's loyal spies.

A Nation Secluded

Since the arrival of the first Westerners in the mid-1500s a number of European traders and Christian missionaries had come to Japan. The Tokugawa distrusted these foreigners. They feared that disloyal daimyo might unite with foreign forces to challenge shogunate rule.

In the early 1600s foreign missionaries and tens of thousands of Japanese Christians were put to death. These brutal measures wiped out Christianity in Japan. The Tokugawa also ended most foreign trade. Only a few Dutch and Chinese traders were allowed contact with selected officials, through one small Kyushu port. New laws made it illegal for any Japanese to leave the country or return to Japan from abroad.

The Tokugawa's seclusion orders isolated Japan from the rest of the world for two centuries. Along with the government's other strict controls,

Merchants and shoppers fill the streets of Edo. In 1868 Edo became the nation's new capital and was renamed Tokyo.

seclusion helped keep the country well ordered and peaceful. Freed from the costs and disruptions of war, Japan's economy grew strong. Business flourished, and city streets bustled with artisans and merchants. Shoppers could buy beautiful fabrics and pottery, elegant swords, and sake (SAH-kee), or rice wine. By the mid-1700s Edo, with more than a million people, had become one of the largest and richest cities in the world.

Over time Japan's strong economy brought changes to its strict social system. Merchants were still considered the lowest class, but many became wealthy and powerful. Even peasants sometimes grew rich by selling silk and other farm products. Meanwhile many cultured and educated samurai, dependent on the small salaries paid by their lords, became poor. Most samurai were forced to borrow money from merchant moneylenders. It was a world turned upside down. Even greater changes were on the horizon.

Opening the Doors

In July 1853 the people of a small Japanese fishing village were terrified by the sight of four black-hulled ships belching smoke and bristling with cannons. The big steam-powered warships puffed into Edo's harbor. Temple bells rang out and merchants hid their valuables. Samurai who had never fought in battle scrubbed the rust from their spears.

The fearsome warships were commanded by Commodore Matthew Perry of the United States. Perry carried a letter from President Millard Fillmore, asking that Japanese ports be opened to American ships. After delivering the letter, Perry sailed away, promising to return the following year for an answer.

Some of the samurai wanted to refuse the Americans' request. Others knew their swords and spears were no match for modern warships and cannons. When Perry returned in 1854, the emperor's officials signed the Treaty of Kanagawa, opening two ports. Within a few years the United States and other nations had bullied Japan

Villagers watch in wonder as Commodore Matthew Perry's black ships arrive in Japan.

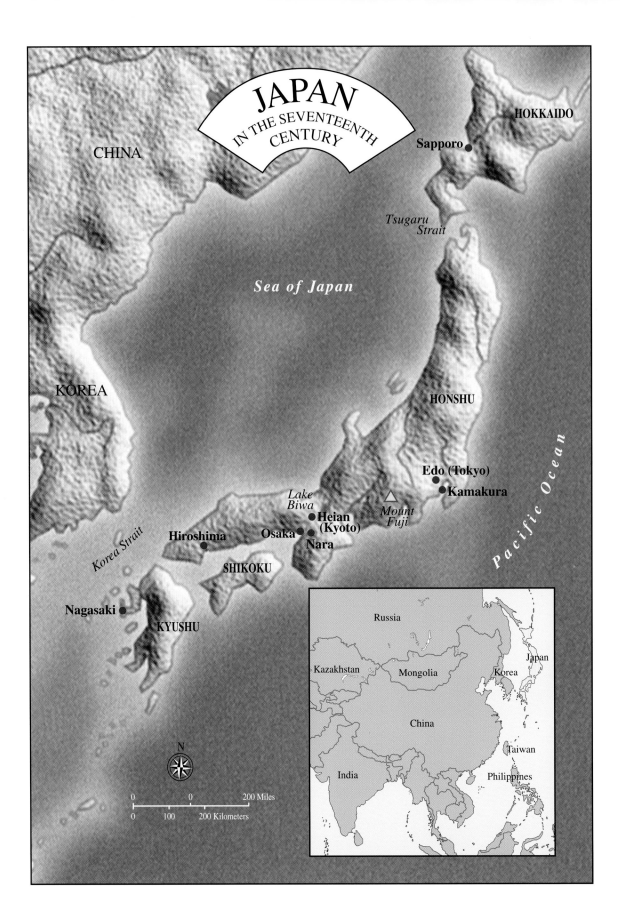

JAPAN
IN THE SEVENTEENTH CENTURY

CHINA

HOKKAIDO

● Sapporo

Tsugaru Strait

Sea of Japan

KOREA

HONSHU

Edo (Tokyo) ●
● Kamakura

Lake Biwa
● Heian (Kyoto)

△ *Mount Fuji*

Osaka ●
● Nara

Korea Strait

Hiroshima ●

SHIKOKU

Nagasaki ●

KYUSHU

Pacific Ocean

N

0   0   200 Miles
0   100   200 Kilometers

Russia

Kazakhstan   Mongolia

Japan

Korea

China

Taiwan

India

Philippines

into signing additional trade agreements. The doors that for so long had been tightly shut against outsiders suddenly were flung wide open.

Soon foreign officials were living in Japan. Most Japanese were horrified. They blamed the shogun for allowing "barbarians" to trample their nation's sacred soil. A group of daimyo joined forces to put an end to shogunate rule. These lords overthrew the Tokugawa. They called for all Japanese to unite under the country's new emperor. As he took the throne, that emperor also took a new name: Meiji, meaning "Enlightened Rule." The end of military government and the emperor's return to power became known as the Meiji Restoration.

In 1868 Emperor Meiji moved the imperial court from Kyoto to the shoguns' capital, Edo, which he renamed Tokyo, or "Eastern Capital." Within a few years of the Meiji Restoration, all the special privileges of the samurai had been outlawed. The age of the samurai warrior was at an end. But the values of the "way of the warrior" survived. These traditions would help shape Japan into a powerful modern nation.

CHAPTER TWO

ARTISTIC TREASURES

Stories of bloody struggles for land and power might make us think of the samurai as no more than fierce warriors. But that is only half the picture. Most samurai were as well trained in literature and other forms of art as they were in warfare. Shoguns and daimyo were great supporters of the arts, encouraging the work of writers, painters, and artisans. Even lower-class samurai were expected to understand and appreciate the beauties of poetry, the theater, flower arranging, the tea ceremony, and more.

Other social classes also made important contributions to art. Members of the imperial court devoted much of their lives to creating and enjoying beauty. Merchants gave Japan some of its most talented playwrights. Artisans built magnificent castles and turned everyday objects into works of outstanding beauty. From all of these gifted hands came a wealth of artistic treasures that captured the spirit of Japanese life in the days of the samurai.

Literature

A Nation of Poets

Japan's earliest form of poetry was the tanka, or "short song." A tanka is an unrhymed poem of five lines, each with a set number of syllables. The Heian Period—the four centuries of Fujiwara rule that began in 794—was a golden

age for Japanese poetry and other literature. The lords and ladies of the Kyoto (Heian) court devoted themselves to tanka writing. They tried to capture, in a few short lines, nature's beauties and the joys and sorrows of love. The following tanka are from

The arts were an important part of life at all levels of Japanese society. In this wood-block print a party of samurai enjoy painting and calligraphy at a teahouse.

twelfth-century collections of poetry assembled by the imperial court:

The cries of the insects
Are buried at the roots of
The sparse pampas grass—
The end of autumn is in
The color of the last leaves.

—The priest Jakuren

Ono no Komachi was a famous beauty and poet who came to court around 840. Thousands of noble ladies lived at the imperial court during the Heian Period, devoting their days to painting and poetry writing.

Whipped by a fierce wind
And dashed like the ocean waves
Against the rocks—
I alone am broken to bits
And now am lost in longing.

—Minamoto no Shigeyuki

After the fall of the Fujiwara clan and the rise of the samurai, many warriors became accomplished poets. A warrior often took as much pride in his talent for poetry writing as he did in his fighting skills. Facing death through war or seppuku, a high-ranking samurai might spend his last moments writing a farewell poem.

A favorite form of poetry among the samurai was the *renga*, or "linked verse." To compose a *renga*, one poet spoke the opening lines of a tanka, then a second completed the poem. Sometimes pairs of poets joined together in *renga* sessions, taking turns to create a chain of one hundred verses.

In the 1600s retired warrior Matsuo Basho became the master of a new type of poem, the haiku (HIE-koo). A haiku has just three lines and seventeen syllables. Many of these short poems present vivid images of nature. In its original Japanese version the first of the following four verses by Basho was considered an example of perfect haiku form.

This ancient pond here:
A frog jumps into the pond:
Sound of the water.

Spring soon ends—
Birds will weep while in
The eyes of fish are tears.

A village where they ring
No bells!—oh, what do they do
At dusk in spring?

Summer grasses—
All that remains
Of a warrior's dreams.

Tales of Love and War

One of the world's greatest novels—many say the world's *first* novel—was written by a court lady in eleventh-century Japan. *The Tale of Genji* by Murasaki Shikibu tells the story of the life and loves of an imaginary prince. More than one thousand pages long, this huge novel offers an inside look at the pleasures and problems of life in the Kyoto court. Other fine literature of the Heian Period includes long, fascinating diaries written by the wives and daughters of court nobles. One of the most famous court diaries, *The Pillow Book* by Sei Shonagon, is full of lively, often funny accounts of events at court.

Following the bloody struggles that ended the Heian Period, Japan's writers turned out stirring tales of war. The greatest collection of war stories was *The Tale of the Heike*. This thirteenth-century work recalls the conflicts between the Taira and Minamoto clans. Along with its glorious accounts of heroic samurai riding into battle, *The Tale of the Heike* reflects on war's sorrows. Some of the most memorable passages recall the death of the boy-emperor Antoku and the loneliness of his grieving mother, whose "tears were never dried."

In the seventeenth century the Tokugawa shoguns brought

A court lady watches her lover depart, in a nineteenth-century wood-block print of a scene from The Tale of Genji. *The novel tells the story of a dashing prince and his romantic adventures in the Kyoto court.*

For much of its early history Japan had no written language. Tales and legends were memorized and passed down by storytellers. Then, in the early fourth century C.E., scholars began to write Japanese using kanji (KAHN-jee), characters borrowed from the Chinese.

Chinese is written in a variety of symbols or characters. Each complicated Chinese character stands for a single word. It was extremely difficult to write Japanese in Chinese characters because the two languages have very different rules of grammar and pronunciation. Only the lords of the royal court were able to spend the years needed to learn how to read and write tens of thousands of kanji.

In the ninth century scholars developed a better way to write Japanese. The new system used kana (KAH-nuh), simpler symbols that stood for sounds instead of whole words. At first noblemen thought that writing kana was beneath them. The ladies of the court, however, welcomed the more sensible system and used kana to write masterpieces in Japanese. In time both men and women adopted the modern style of writing Japanese, which uses kana, kanji, and other characters.

Each character in Japanese is formed by up to a dozen different brushstrokes. That makes fine writing as beautiful to look at as it is to read. In the days of the samurai, writing with brush and ink became an honored art form, called calligraphy. Well-educated nobles and warriors spent many hours practicing their handwriting. Graceful writing was so prized that when the imperial court sank into poverty during the Age of the Country at War, the emperor was able to support himself by selling samples of his calligraphy.

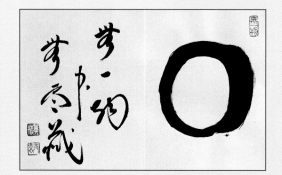

Calligraphy is the art of fine writing with brush and ink.

peace. Writers lost interest in warriors and focused instead on the rising merchant class. Ihara Saikaku, a novelist and Osaka merchant, set his lighthearted tales in city streets and shops. In *The Eternal Storehouse of Japan*, Saikaku's hero is a wealthy but cheap shop owner. When guests visit the rich man's home, they hear sounds in the kitchen and look forward to a feast. Their host, however, announces that no meal will be served. "Not to provide refreshments is one way of becoming a millionaire," he explains. "The noise . . . which you heard when you first arrived was the pounding of starch for the covers of the account book."

On the Stage

When shogun Tokugawa Ieyasu invited Japan's leading daimyo to his castle in Edo, he often entertained them with a performance of Noh. This elegant form of drama, which began in the 1300s, was the only type of public entertainment considered dignified enough for a samurai. Noh plays told stories from ancient Japanese legends. The characters included ghosts, spirits, and demons. Noh actors—all men—wore splendid costumes and masks. Accompanied by the chanting of poetry and the music of a flute and drums, they performed slow, silent, measured dance steps. Each graceful gesture the actors made had a correct form and special meaning. Gently moving a sleeve in a certain way, for example, meant a character was falling in love.

The mood of a Noh play was solemn and mysterious. A Kabuki (kuh-BOO-kee) performance was quite a different show. Kabuki developed in the 1600s and was meant for merchants and other ordinary townspeople. Performances were loud and

Noh plays were performed on a bare stage contrasting with the splendid costumes and masks worn by the actors. A chanting chorus, shown to the left, commented on the action.

Two actors perform in a Kabuki play. This wood-block print was made by Utagawa Kunisada, an eighteenth-century artist who specialized in scenes from the theater.

action-packed, with plots often based on current events. The actors wore colorful costumes, heavy makeup, and wigs. Dancing and striding with exaggerated movements, they sang, made dramatic speeches, fought daring duels, and were magically transformed into dragons and other fantastic creatures. The Tokugawa shoguns thought Kabuki was vulgar. They banned women from acting and tried several times to ban Kabuki completely. But its popularity among both the samurai and the lower classes kept this exciting form of drama alive.

Another popular Japanese dramatic art was Bunraku (bun-RAH-koo), or puppet theater. Bunraku was very much like Kabuki, except that the "actors" were large wooden puppets. Three puppeteers dressed in black operated each nearly life-size doll, producing amazingly realistic action. Chikamatsu Monzaemon wrote masterful plays for Bunraku. Audiences were moved to tears as the wooden figures seemed to come alive in his stories of heroism and doomed love.

Paint and Ink

A warrior's frustration led to the creation of one of Japan's most famous paintings. In 1281, after the Mongol invasions, samurai grumbled about the small payments awarded for their brave fighting. One warrior hired artists to create a narrative scroll—a painting made on a long roll of paper that tells a story as it is unrolled—about his exploits in battle and his meager rewards. The Mongol Invasion Scroll is rich with grand action and tiny details that give us much information about samurai dress, weapons, and fighting styles.

Japan had learned the art of narrative scroll painting during its early contacts with China. The first Japanese scrolls showed religious subjects such as episodes from the lives of holy people. Later subjects included brightly painted scenes from nature, court or city life, and great battles. Japanese artists also painted on hanging scrolls and on screens or panels made of paper or silk, used to divide and decorate rooms.

In the 1300s many of Japan's artists adopted the Chinese painting style called *sumi-e* (SOO-mee-eh). Using delicate brushstrokes, *sumi-e* artists painted simple landscapes almost entirely in black ink.

Two centuries later Oda Nobunaga seized control of much of Japan. To decorate his magnificent new castle, the warlord commanded Japan's best painters to create dazzling designs. Other daimyo, eager to show off their own wealth and importance, copied Nobunaga's splashy style. Soon artists across Japan were creating scrolls and screens bursting with brilliant watercolors and glittering with flakes of gold.

Under the Tokugawa shoguns the artists' best customers were wealthy townspeople. Merchants were so eager for art that painters began to use

carved wooden blocks dipped in ink to make copies of their best works. Some artists created wood-block prints showing scenes of everyday city life. Other popular subjects included Kabuki players, fierce-looking samurai, and geisha (GAY-shuh), lovely women trained in the arts of conversation and hospitality.

This colorful six-fold screen, painted with dramatic scenes of battle, may have graced the home of a wealthy Japanese merchant or samurai.

The traditional art of ikebana still brings beauty to Japanese homes.

Flowers and Gardens

In samurai Japan artistry was not only for artists. All Japanese appreciated the natural beauties of their country and tried to bring a part of that beauty into their daily lives. Most homes were decorated with flowers—not big bouquets but single blossoms or a graceful flowering branch. Many people studied the art of ikebana (ih-kay-BAH-nuh), or flower arranging. They learned to select and display flowers and twigs according to strict rules of color, grouping, and shape. The perfect flower arrangement was more than a thing of beauty. Because each group of leaves and bend of twig had a specific religious meaning, ikebana also enriched the mind and spirit.

A spiritual meaning could be found in Japanese gardens, too. Every samurai home had a soothing, artistically designed garden that served as a hideaway for thought and prayer. Larger gardens might include flowers and shrubs, wooded groves, shaded paths, fountains, and ponds with golden fish darting in and out of cool rock caves. Also popular were rock and sand gardens. These mysterious arrangements of rocks, raked pebbles, and sand always carried a hidden message. At one of the most famous rock and sand gardens, the Daisen-in of Kyoto, a tumbling stream of sand tells the story of a soul's journey through the obstacles of life.

Everyday Art

Many of Japan's arts and crafts were borrowed from the Chinese. Over time Japanese artisans added their own production methods and designs. They used their perfected skills to turn everyday objects into works of art.

Beautiful bowls and dishes, wine bottles, cosmetic boxes, and other household items were crafted of lacquerware. Japanese lacquer was made by adding coloring—usually red or black—to tree sap. Artisans painted many layers of lacquer onto wood or paper to create a hard, shiny surface, which they often decorated with gold.

Japanese artisans also made pottery and porcelain of exceptional quality and beauty. A samurai might value an elegant earthenware tea bowl made by a famous artisan as much as his finest sword.

Swordsmiths were among Japan's most respected artisans. In a country so often at war, the warrior's chief weapon had to be strong and razor-sharp. Shaping and heating steel to make the blade was a difficult, complicated process. Just as important was the design of a sword's beautiful fittings—its scabbard, hilt (handle), and hand guard. Made of copper or other metals, the fittings were richly decorated with jewels, lacquer, or designs traced in ivory or gold.

Armor was also beautifully decorated, often with lacquer or painted designs. The crowning glory was the helmet. High-ranking samurai wore helmets topped with painted wooden horns or other extravagant ornaments so that their exploits in battle would not go unnoticed. Some warriors also wore ferocious-looking face masks to strike terror in the hearts of the enemy.

The samurai wore small, handsomely decorated lacquer medicine boxes called inro *on cords hanging from the sashes of their robes. This* inro *shows a servant kneeling before a samurai.*

Samurai Castles

The samurai castle is the grandest example of the blending of beauty and practicality in the Japanese arts. Japan's castles were among the most beautiful buildings in the world, yet every detail of their design was planned for defense.

The first samurai castles were rough wooden forts set beside rivers and swamps or on hilltops and rocky cliffs. Protected by natural defenses, these forts sheltered samurai bands fighting to

THE TEA CEREMONY

After slicing off enemy heads in battle, sixteenth-century warlord Toyotomi Hideyoshi enjoyed nothing more than relaxing with friends over a bowl of ceremonial tea. The custom of drinking tea as part of a religious ceremony had come to Japan from Korea and China during the Heian Period. In time the tea ceremony became a form of art highly valued by the samurai. Mastering the rituals surrounding the making and serving of tea was an honored accomplishment, and practicing the ceremony showed a warrior's exquisite taste and manners.

The tea ceremony was held in a teahouse—a simple building set in a beautiful garden. The softly colored tea bowl, serving utensils, vases, and other articles of the ceremony were made from plain, natural materials. An elaborate code of rules governed every step of the long ceremony. There was a proper way for the host to prepare and serve the tea and for guests to enter the teahouse, to sit and speak, to pass the drinking bowl. Through the quiet enjoyment of all these rituals, the weary samurai entered an island of peace. "Our mental dust is wiped off," said one master of the art, and "we . . . become oblivious to all worldly woes and worries."

defend a lord's estate or conquer neighboring lands.

By the end of the sixteenth century daimyo ruled over their private domains. A daimyo's castle served not only as a base for fighting but also as the political and economic center of his domain. Because most castles were located along main trade routes, on sites with no natural protection, they had to have their own built-in defenses. They also had to be large enough to hold an entire army in wartime and grand enough to show off their owner's wealth and importance.

Daimyo castles were built on large earth mounds covered with blocks of stone. Crowning this tall foundation was the main building, or keep. Made of wood, the keep might be several stories high. Curving tile roofs and elegant decorations gave it a fairy-tale loveliness. The walls of

The Castle of the White Heron in the town of Himeji is one of the most magnificent surviving daimyo fortresses.

the keep might be covered with shiny black lacquer or decorated with gold. Himeji Castle, built by Toyotomi Hideyoshi, was coated with white fireproof plaster, earning it the nickname Castle of the White Heron.

Inside the castle's keep a daimyo and his family lived in comfort and elegance. Painted screens brightened their rooms, and the ceilings were carved and painted with colorful designs. Tables, chests, vases, and other furnishings were made of the finest materials, crafted by Japan's best artisans.

Amid all this beauty and luxury, castles bristled with defenses. Through trapdoors in the stone foundation, defenders could dump rocks on attackers. The keep's windows were barred, and doors had iron locks and bolts. Slits in the walls let hidden defenders shoot guns and arrows, and charming balconies served as shooting platforms. The buildings and grounds were surrounded by rows of stone walls and water-filled moats. For attackers who managed to get through these outer defenses, there was a special greeting: a bath of boiling liquids poured through holes above the castle's gates.

The Castle Town

Samurai lived in the shadow of their daimyo's castle, in simple houses built of wood and thatch. This house belonged to a samurai family named Hakogi.

Surrounding a daimyo's castle were the homes of his followers. The most important samurai had houses near the keep. Lower-ranking warriors lived outside the castle walls, grouped in neighborhoods according to their rank. Between the higher and lower

samurai were areas set aside for favored merchants and artisans. Outside the borders of the castle town lay the fields and the dark, cramped huts of the peasant farmers.

The size of a samurai's house depended on his rank, but all shared the same basic design. Built of wood, houses had sloping roofs covered with thatch, shingles, or tiles. The floors were raised off the ground to keep the house dry during the rainy season. Inside, there were no permanent walls. Instead rooms were divided by wall panels that slid along grooves in the floor. Painted screens also could be arranged to create private spots.

Samurai homes had little furniture: only a few cushions, tables, and storage chests made of wood and woven vines. Because everyone sat or knelt on the floor, chests and tables were built low. The floors were covered with rectangular straw mats called tatami (tah-TAH-mee). People slept on cotton-filled cloth mats, which were rolled up and stored during the day. The man of the house slept on the thickest mattress, sometimes surrounded by curtains.

Even the lowest-ranking samurai was master in his own house. His wife and children were expected to show him respect and obedience. A samurai spent most of his time away from home. In periods of war he followed his lord into battle. In peacetime he worked a long day, serving his daimyo at the castle or about town. When the workday ended, a warrior might relax at a bathhouse or drink sake with samurai friends. Sometimes he hid his face behind a basketlike hat to attend an entertaining but improper Kabuki show.

Other popular samurai pastimes exercised the body, mind, and senses. Warriors enjoyed hunting, swimming, and training in the martial arts. They wrote poetry, practiced flower arranging and the tea ceremony, and played go, a board game with black and white stones. At incense-burning competitions, they tried to guess the greatest number of incense smells. Nature's beauties were the attraction at moon-viewing and snow-viewing parties. Spring was the season for blossom viewing. As they gathered to admire the blossoms of the cherry tree, the samurai reflected on the rich but often tragically short life of a Japanese warrior.

CHAPTER THREE

"LAND OF THE GODS"

Gazing down from the heavenly plains, the god Izanagi and goddess Izanami create Japan.

Supernatural beings who made their homes in mountains and storms. A wise prince who taught that meditation was the key to happiness. These are the central beings of two different religions, Shinto and Buddhism (BOO-diz-um). The first began in ancient Japan, while the second had its roots in ancient India. In the days of the samurai the Japanese combined the beliefs and practices of the two faiths. Like many other aspects of its culture, Japan's religion became a blend of foreign and native ideas that was uniquely Japanese.

Shinto: "The Way of the Gods"

The early Japanese worshiped the mysterious forces and forms of nature. Out of their practices came the religion of Shinto, or "the way of the gods."

Shinto was a simple faith with deep meaning for its followers. It had no holy writings or moral rules, but it inspired a great reverence for all of nature. Followers of Shinto believed that spirits called *kami* (KAH-mee) lived in many of nature's wonders. The sacred homes of *kami* included mountains, trees, lakes, rivers, streams, waterfalls, islands, and oddly shaped rocks.

An eighteenth-century Shinto scholar described *kami* as including "such objects as birds, beasts, trees, plants, seas, mountains, and so forth. In ancient times, anything whatsoever which was outside the ordinary, which possessed superior powers, or which was awe-inspiring was called *kami*."

Shinto followers also worshiped a number of gods and goddesses. These supernatural beings had power over the winds, the tides, and other natural forces. The most important deity was the sun goddess Amaterasu, daughter of the gods who created Japan. According to legend, Japan's emperors were descended from Amaterasu. That made the emperors *kami*, too.

The host of *kami* was always growing, because it included ancestor spirits. When warriors and other important family members died, their spirits were believed to live on. To honor their ancestors and other *kami*, the Japanese visited Shinto shrines.

Every village had a simple wooden shrine with an entrance marked by a torii (TOHR-ee-ee)—a sacred gateway topped by one straight and one curving beam. More than just a house of worship, the shrine was a gathering place for spirits. Visitors clapped their hands to get the spirits' attention and offered small gifts of rice and sake. Sometimes they prayed to a *kami* for advice and protection. Girls who were about to marry, women expecting babies, and warriors setting out for battle said special prayers. In large shrines priests helped carry people's prayers to the spirits by chanting Shinto hymns and performing dances.

Priests also helped people purify themselves through Shinto rituals. One of the most important elements of Shinto was cleanliness. This meant more than just washing up before entering a shrine. Illness, a death in the family, childbirth, and many other acts and events brought impurity. After a death the remaining family members had to be purified through Shinto rituals. When a baby was born, the new mother and her home were cleansed with a sprinkling of sacred salt.

The famous Floating Torii, or gateway, leads to the Shinto shrine at Miyajima Island. The heart of the Shinto religion is a reverence for nature, so torii are designed to harmonize with the natural landscape.

Ancient Japanese songs and legends describe the creation of the world. The god Izanagi and the goddess Izanami dipped a spear into the ocean. From the tip of the spear drops of water fell to earth. The drops became the islands of Japan.

Izanagi and Izanami created many *kami* to manage their beautiful islands. They gave their children power over the mountains and rivers, seas and storms. Then, according to an eighth-century chronicle, the divine couple "consulted together, saying, 'We have now produced the Great-eight-island country, with the mountains, rivers, herbs, and trees. Why should we not produce someone who shall be lord of the universe?' They then together produced the sun goddess, who was called Amaterasu."

In time Amaterasu sent her grandson, Ninigi, to rule over her islands. To prove that Ninigi was divine, the goddess gave him three treasures: a sacred mirror, an iron sword, and a curved jewel. In 660 B.C.E. Ninigi's great-grandson Jimmu Tenno, or "The Divine Warrior," became the first human emperor of Japan.

The story of Amaterasu and Jimmu is myth, but like most ancient tales it has elements of fact. Many historians believe that Jimmu was one of Japan's early leaders, though he probably ruled six to eight centuries later than the dates given in the chronicles. Amaterasu's gifts to her divine grandson remain important symbols in Japan. The regalia—a mirror, sword, and jewels—have long been considered proof of the imperial family's right to rule. Throughout Japan's history emperors fleeing from war have taken the regalia with them into hiding. Today the regalia jewels are housed at the Imperial Palace in Tokyo, and the mirror and sword are in two separate Shinto shrines.

Buddhism: The Path to Enlightenment

In the early sixth century C.E. travelers from Korea brought the Buddhist religion to Japan. Founded in India more than nine hundred years earlier, Buddhism was widely practiced in Korea, China, and much of the rest of Asia. The faith's founder, an Indian prince known as the Buddha, or "Enlightened One," did not call for the worship of any particular deities. Instead he taught that all human unhappiness was caused by desire. Desire could be overcome by following the Eightfold Noble Path of right understanding, right thought, right speech, right action, right livelihood, right moral effort, right mindfulness, and right concentration. The path would bring followers to a state of enlightenment (total knowledge) and endless happiness called nirvana.

At first most Shinto followers rejected Buddhism. The powerful Soga clan, however, saw the religion as a source of new and powerful magic. When the Soga's Prince Shotoku became regent to the empress in 593, he built Buddhist temples all across Japan. Many Japanese converted to Buddhism. They admired the art and ceremony that surrounded the new religion—the beautifully ornamented temples, the richly robed priests, the lacquer boxes holding sacred writings. Buddhism also filled a hole left by Japan's ancient faith. Unlike Shinto, the new religion offered rules of right and wrong and guidelines for proper behavior.

Soon the rivalry between Buddhism and Shinto ended.

Prince Shotoku poses with two attendants. The prince introduced many new ideas to Japanese government and society, including the religion of Buddhism.

Preserving what they liked from each faith, the Japanese practiced the two religions side by side. They honored their Shinto gods and goddesses, nature spirits, and ancestors by visiting both temples and shrines. They tried to lead a good life by following Buddhism's moral rules and guidance. Many people showed reverence for their Shinto *kami* by displaying a statue of the Buddha, purchased from the local shrine, in a place of honor in their homes.

Death was another occasion for combining Shinto and Buddhist beliefs and practices. When a person died, the family followed the Buddhist custom of cremating (burning) the body and burying the ashes at a Buddhist temple. The dead person's spirit entered the cycle of reincarnation, or rebirth. Buddhism taught that spirits were reincarnated again and again, with their behavior in each life determining their happiness in the next. Only people who overcame all human desires and reached nirvana could escape the endless cycle of death and rebirth.

In Japan's blending of Shinto and Buddhism, spirits did not simply wait in the temple for reincarnation. Thirty-three years after death a person's spirit moved from the temple to a Shinto shrine. Through Shinto ceremonies the spirit was formally welcomed, or enshrined. A spirit that was not properly enshrined might become an angry ghost and cause trouble among the living.

Two Forms of Buddhism

In the Japanese movie *The Seven Samurai*, warriors hoping to be chosen for a special task are told to walk through a doorway. A young man hides behind the door, holding a big stick. Some warriors are hit, while others manage to dodge the attacker. The very best warriors, sensing the nearness of danger, refuse to pass through the door.

One of the ways expert samurai developed an almost supernatural awareness of their surroundings was through the practice of Zen Buddhism. By the days of the samurai, Buddhism had developed a number of different divisions, or sects, in Japan. The most popular sect among the warrior class was Zen. This practical form of religion emphasized self-discipline and self-reliance. Followers learned to control their bodies through harsh physical training. They strengthened their minds and spirits through meditation. To meditate, a samurai sat cross-legged and motionless for hours, with his mind cleared of all thoughts and desires. In

this way he hoped to find inner peace and enlightenment.

Some samurai thought that Zen Buddhism was too strict and demanding. Many of these warriors preferred the Pure Land sect, which was based on faith in Lord Amida, the Buddha of Boundless Light. Amidists believed that their Buddhist lord had founded a paradise above the clouds. To get there, all they had to do was have faith in Amida and chant his name in prayer. Amidist warriors were especially fierce and fearless fighters, because they rode into battle believing that death meant instant entry into heaven.

The rock garden at Kyoto's Ryoanji Temple has fascinated visitors for centuries. To some, the Zen-inspired garden represents a majestic seascape, while others see mountaintops above the clouds.

Confucianism: The Key to Harmony

Along with Buddhism, a set of beliefs called Confucianism made its way to Japan in the sixth century. Based on the teachings of the ancient Chinese wise man Confucius, this philosophy stressed the importance of duty and proper behavior. Confucianism said that government had a responsibility to provide good, kindhearted leadership. At the same time people should show loyalty to their leaders, respect to those higher on the social scale, and kindness to those below.

Festivals offered a special chance for the Japanese to celebrate their religious heritage. The most important festival was Bon. During this lively midsummer celebration, ancestor spirits visited their families. Graves were cleaned and decorated with flowers to welcome the spirits. Statues of a Buddhist saint who was believed to serve as adviser to the dead were scrubbed and covered with flower garlands. Merrymakers entertained their visiting ancestors with a three-day party of dances, disguises, and fireworks. At the end of the festival lanterns were floated on the water to light the spirits' journey back to their sacred homes.

Shichi-go-san (shee-chee goh sahn), or "Seven Five Three" Day, was a quieter festival, meant especially for children. Since ancient times the numbers seven, five, and three had been considered unlucky. At Shichi-go-san, boys and girls who were three years old, boys who were five, and girls who were seven dressed in their best clothes and went to the local Shinto shrine. Their parents gave thanks for the children's health and asked the spirits for continuing good fortune.

The festival of Tanabata, or "Seventh Evening," also dated from ancient times. In a grand parade of painted lanterns and pounding drums, villagers carried a large box to a river or stream. Inside the box were messages, which were cast into the water, to the river god or to a Shinto river princess and the shepherd boy she loved. Ancient tales said that the lovers had been separated by the princess's father, the King of the Sky. They were allowed to meet only once a year, on opposite sides of the Milky Way. At festival time, in early July, the Milky Way looked like a flowing white river in the sky. According to the tale, birds magically formed a bridge across the river so the lovers could defy the King of the Sky and be reunited.

Though Tanabata was a Shinto festival, Buddhists joyfully joined the festivities. For these Japanese, honoring Shinto deities was just another way to celebrate their faith in the Buddha and his teachings.

For several centuries Buddhism overshadowed Confucianism. Then, under the Tokugawa shoguns, from the seventeenth to mid–nineteenth centuries, the ancient teachings of Confucius found new life. The samurai embraced the Confucian belief that each person had a specific role in society and a sacred duty to fulfill that role. To ensure that all Japanese lived in harmony, the young had a duty to respect their elders, wives to obey their husbands, and children to obey their parents. All citizens owed their government absolute loyalty. In turn, government had to be honest, kind, and efficient.

The warrior's special responsibility was to give his lord loyalty and service. His high position in society also meant that he must balance his military skills with learning and an appreciation of the arts. During the Tokugawa period a samurai who studied Japan's ancient literature and supported the arts was considered a true Confucian gentleman.

Christianity: The Persecuted Faith

In 1549, just a few years after Westerners brought the first guns to Japan, missionaries stepped ashore to spread the Christian religion. They were led by the Catholic priest Frances Xavier. Xavier and his men received a warm welcome from Oda Nobunaga. To Japan's leading warlord, Christianity seemed a handy tool for challenging enemies in powerful Buddhist sects.

Under Nobunaga's protection, the priests began preaching to the samurai, who admired the missionaries' courage and self-discipline. Many daimyo and other high-ranking samurai converted to the new faith. Once they converted, their followers usually did, too. By 1582 there were more than 150,000 Japanese Christians.

In spite of Christianity's rapid acceptance, many Japanese distrusted the new religion. They could not understand the priests' insistence that all faiths but Christianity were wrong. The missionaries made enemies by attacking Japan's other religions and destroying ancient Shinto shrines. Sometimes they forced a Christian daimyo's followers to convert. A few missionaries became alarmingly powerful. One wealthy daimyo who converted to Christianity showed his devotion to his new faith by turning over control of the port city of Nagasaki to the missionaries. The priest who became ruler of that rich city offended many samurai by traveling along Japan's coastline in a huge, well-armed warship.

In 1587 Toyotomi Hideyoshi, the warlord who united Japan after the Age of the Country at War, declared that Christianity was an "outrageous" insult to the "land of the Gods." Three decades later shogun Tokugawa Ieyasu issued an order banning Christianity.

Following Ieyasu's death other Tokugawa shoguns brutally enforced his order. Priests who refused to leave the country were beaten, imprisoned, and sometimes put to death. Tens of thousands of Japanese Christians were tortured. A Dutch merchant who visited Japan in the early 1600s wrote that he saw Christians "being scalded with boiling water, burnt with red-hot irons, beaten with lashes, left stark naked for whole days in the heat of the sun by day and the cold by night." By the 1660s the land that embraced both Shinto and Buddhism had swept away every trace of Christianity.

CHAPTER FOUR

A CULTURE SHAPED BY FAITH

From the daimyo's castle to the artisan's workshop to the peasant's simple farmhouse—in every corner of samurai Japan, the gods were near. Religion was a natural part of everyday life for the Japanese. It shaped the country's government and arts, and it influenced the way people lived, fought, and died.

The sun goddess Amaterasu shines in a wood-block print by Kunisada. According to legend, Japan's emperors were descended from Amaterasu, who emerged from a cave to give the world light.

The Gods in Government

For more than fifteen hundred years Japan's system of government was rooted in the Shinto faith. The imperial family's right to rule came from the sun goddess Amaterasu herself. A long, unbroken line of emperors and empresses served not only as the formal heads of government but also as the country's highest priests. No warlord, no matter how ambitious, ever dared to challenge these half-human, half-divine rulers.

But ambitious leaders did find a way to take the real power out of imperial hands. The shoguns were especially skillful at using Shinto beliefs as the foundation for their form of government. In shogunate rule the shogun was the country's political leader, the emperor its spiritual

head. Taking over the responsibility of running the country, the shoguns respectfully issued orders in the emperor's name. Meanwhile the sacred imperial rulers were left with only one duty—to ensure Japan's good fortune by performing Shinto rituals and ceremonies at court.

The ancient myths that made the emperor a sacred being gave ordinary Japanese people a sense of their own unique importance. The gods and goddesses of the old tales had favored Japan above all other places on earth. They had filled its lands, seas, and skies with powerful spirits to watch over their beloved people. In the late thirteenth century, when Mongol invaders were driven off by a "divine wind," the Japanese took it as proof that they were the gods' favored people. This belief inspired them to treasure their native culture and guard it against foreign influences. In the seventeenth century the Tokugawa shoguns took that national pride to the extreme when they issued orders that cut off contact with the outside world for two hundred years.

Buddhism and the Arts

By the time Buddhism reached Japan in the sixth century, it was already more than nine hundred years old. Through the religion's long history its followers had created a rich body of literature, art, and ideas. Prince Shotoku, who became regent to the empress in 593, was eager to bring these cultural riches to Japan. Shotoku sent scholars to China to learn from that country's great culture. Some studied Chinese laws and politics, gathering ideas that Shotoku used to redesign Japan's government. Others visited Buddhist temples and monasteries (retreats for monks) and studied the faith's holy writings. The knowledge these scholars brought back to Japan completely transformed their country's arts.

Buddhist writings inspired the beginning of written literature in Japan. The artwork of Buddhist temples encouraged the adoption of narrative scroll painting as well as advances in lacquerware, metalworking, and architecture. In the early 700s a new Japanese capital was built at Nara, with streets and court buildings modeled after those in the Chinese capital. Elsewhere in Japan, Buddhist monasteries and temples were built in the Chinese style. The richly ornamented temples had elaborate tile roofs held up by thick pillars. Inside they were filled with glittering bronze bells, lacquer altars, decorative metalwork, paintings, and statues. The

IF YOU LIVED IN SAMURAI JAPAN

If you had been born during the days of the samurai, your way of life would have been determined by your social class and whether you were female or male. This chart traces the course your life might have taken as a boy or girl in a samurai family.

You were born in Edo. . . .

As a Boy . . .

As a Girl . . .

Your birth is a cause for great celebration. When you are a month old, your mother takes you to the local Shinto shrine to give thanks and ask for the *kami*'s continuing protection. Your parents love and pamper you but teach you to respect your elders and always behave properly.

At age 7 you dress in your first *hakama*, a pair of wide trousers worn over a kimono. You visit the shrine to tell the *kami* that you have passed from babyhood to childhood. You learn how to ride horseback and use a small bow and wooden sword.

At age 7 you wear your first long kimono, tied around the waist with a colorful sash. You visit the shrine to tell the *kami* that you have passed from babyhood to childhood.

At age 10 you may go to a Buddhist monastery or samurai training school. You work hard learning to read and write, studying Chinese classics, and training with sword, spear, and bow.

From ages 7 to 12 or 13 you help your mother at home, doing household chores and taking care of your younger brothers and sisters. Your mother teaches you a little reading and writing, proper behavior and dress, and the arts of ikebana and the tea ceremony.

At about age 14 the front part of your head is shaved as a sign that you have become a man. You are given a steel sword and a suit of armor. Now you are ready to fight in battle.

At age 12 or 13 your eyebrows are plucked until only a thin arch remains. This ceremony marks your passage into womanhood. Soon your parents will choose a husband for you, and you will move into his family's home.

As a warrior you follow your lord into battle. In peacetime you work at his castle or in town and spend most evenings relaxing with samurai friends.

As a wife and mother you spend most of your time at home. You care for the children, manage the household, and keep track of expenses. You also may train in the martial arts.

Few warriors live a long life. If you manage to survive into old age, you retire from fighting but are still treated with great respect.

In old age you live a quiet life. If your husband has died, you may live with your son's family or become a Buddhist nun and live in a convent.

When you die, your body is cremated. The ashes are buried at a Buddhist temple, and your spirit may be enshrined at the local Shinto shrine.

Tens of thousands of Japanese visit the majestic bronze Buddha of Kamakura each year. The forty-two-foot statue was created in 1252, six centuries after Buddhism was introduced to Japan.

Todaiji Temple, built at Nara in the 740s, housed a fifty-foot-tall statue of the Buddha. Japanese artisans labored for fourteen years to create this awe-inspiring image. Made largely of copper, the statue is covered with five hundred pounds of gold.

In the twelfth century a second cultural wave grew up around a new Buddhist sect called Zen. Zen Buddhism taught self-discipline, simplicity, and meditation as paths to inner peace. Zen arts were meant to help followers in their journey along those paths. Gardens at Buddhist temples and samurai homes were designed as aids to meditation. Through the artistic placement of shrubs, flowers, ponds, and fountains, living gardens created a feeling of peace and harmony with nature. At rock and sand gardens monks and samurai spent hours meditating on the spiritual message hidden in the arrangements of rocks, pebbles, and sand.

The art of ikebana (flower arranging) also had religious significance. Each leaf, twig, and flower stood for truth, understanding, or some other element of Buddhist thought. By creating and enjoying flower arrangements, the Japanese expressed both their love of nature and their desire for religious enlightenment.

Many other forms of Japanese art reflected the simplicity and discipline of Zen. *Sumi-e* painting captured the beauties of nature through a few simple strokes of black ink. The tea ceremony,

Sumi-e *paintings reflect the Zen philosophy in simple strokes of ink expressing nature's beauty and harmony. This painting by* sumi-e *artist Mu-ch'i is titled* Six Persimmons.

introduced to Japan by Chinese Buddhist monks, was a symbol of self-control and tranquillity. The actions of the tea host and guests were graceful and calming. The tea bowls, plates, and vases had a plain, natural beauty. Mastering the strict rules surrounding the rituals of the ceremony took the dedication and self-discipline of a true Zen scholar.

Zen and Samurai Ideals

Samurai were the most enthusiastic followers of Zen in Japan. Shinto had already taught these warriors that death was simply a passage to the world of the *kami*. Zen promised to strengthen their minds and spirits to help them face that journey with calmness and self-assurance. By teaching a samurai how to control his mind during combat, Zen also could improve his fighting skills and help him delay his final passage.

During the Tokugawa period, Zen masters opened schools of swordsmanship, archery, and other martial arts. They taught the importance of fighting in a Zen state of mind. A samurai who reached that state was able to clear his mind of all thoughts and fears, enabling him to fight in an unplanned, natural style.

Yagyu Matajuro was a samurai boy who learned the Zen state of mind through an unusual course of study. When Matajuro begged the famous swordsman Banzo to teach him the art of swordsmanship, the man agreed. The boy moved into the master's home. One night, while Matajuro was sleeping, Banzo hit him with a wooden sword. From then on, the boy never knew when to expect a surprise attack. Over time he learned how to sense unseen danger and avoid his master's stick. Matajuro had not taken a single formal lesson, but Banzo sent him home with a fine new sword and a certificate of mastery.

The Cultured Confucian Warrior

The teachings of the Chinese philosopher Confucius played a major role in shaping Japanese beliefs and customs. Confucianism taught that government should be strong, honest, and efficient. The Fujiwara regents who transformed Japan's government in the seventh and eighth centuries based many of their changes on that Confucian ideal.

Confucianism also taught that respect and loyalty were the keys to a peaceful society. Each person owed respectful obedience to those higher on the social scale, kindness and protection to those below. In Japan's feudal age that rule became the heart of the relationship between lords and vassals. It also contributed to the code of loyalty that was the first rule of Bushido.

Under the Tokugawa shoguns a rebirth of interest in Confucianism dealt a blow to the status of women in Japanese society. According to Confucian thinking, each person had a strictly defined role. A woman's role was to serve and obey her husband. The samurai's embrace of that

SAMURAI WOMEN

The most famous samurai woman in Japanese history was Tomoe Gozen, wife of the powerful general Minamoto Yoshinaka. In 1184, toward the end of the Gempei War between the Taira and Minamoto clans, Yoshinaka's forces fought a fierce battle. The enemy was stronger. Yoshinaka's men prepared for one final charge. *The Tale of the Heike* recalls how Tomoe refused to leave her husband, declaring, "I want to fight the last glorious fight in front of you." When an enemy warrior approached, Tomoe "dragged him from his horse . . . and cut off his head." Yoshinaka was killed during the fighting, and Tomoe spent the rest of her life at a Buddhist convent, reciting prayers for his spirit.

Many other samurai women trained in the martial arts. Some became skilled fighters who showed the same courage and loyalty as samurai men. In the early days of the samurai, women also were highly respected for their ability to manage their households and raise their children. Part of women's power came from their right to inherit property and pass it on to their children.

Between the thirteenth and seventeenth centuries women's status slowly sank. The idea that women were inferior to men became an accepted rule of life in Japan. Young women became tools for increasing a family's wealth and importance through marriage. A samurai wife was expected to meekly serve and obey her husband and bear sons to inherit his property.

Despite their lowly status, samurai women still had important responsibilities at home. They handled the household expenses, managed the servants, and taught their children the ideals of Bushido and Buddhism. Wives showed their husbands the same devotion a warrior showed his lord. Sometimes that included fighting to defend their home and honor and committing seppuku in the face of defeat.

Two samurai women practice fighting with wooden staffs called jo. *Although Japanese society was dominated by men, women often trained in the martial arts, becoming highly skilled fighters.*

belief took away many of the rights and freedoms women had enjoyed in earlier centuries.

The Tokugawa period also saw a flowering of the arts, largely inspired by Confucian teachings. One of a samurai's duties, according to Confucianism, was to serve as a role model for the rest of society. He was to fulfill that duty by balancing his martial skills with more peaceful accomplishments. Warriors of this period studied ancient Japanese literature and supported the work of skilled artists and artisans. They wrote poetry, painted, and practiced the tea ceremony. A seventeenth-century book on correct samurai behavior summed up the attitude of warriors who "take up verse making or Teaism. . . . Though Bushido naturally implies first of all the qualities of strength and forcefulness, to have this one side only developed is to be nothing but a rustic [unsophisticated] samurai of no great account."

CHAPTER FIVE

THE LIVING SAMURAI SPIRIT

It would be surprising if a group of people as powerful and productive as the samurai vanished without a trace. Though the reforms following the Meiji Restoration put an end to the warrior class, the spirit of the samurai lived on. Samurai ideals and traditions guided the growth of modern Japan and still influence its economy and society. In fact, the samurai spirit touches more lives today than ever before, because its influence reaches outside Japan to many other parts of the world.

Dreams of Empire

Some samurai fought against the Meiji reforms, but most realized that their country had to change in order to survive in the modern world. As Japan's best-educated people, these former samurai led the nation in a rapid program of modernization. Just a few decades after the end of shogunate rule, new factories, railways, and schools had completely transformed Japanese business, transportation, and education. Another major target of modernization was Japan's military. The Japanese were determined to replace their old-fashioned fighting forces with an army strong enough to compete with the rest of the world.

By 1894 Japan had become a world-class military power. Backing up its modern weapons and fighting methods was the ancient Shinto belief in the superiority of the Japanese people. Military leaders were convinced that Japan was destined to rule the world. They began a brutal program of conquest, battling Chinese and Russian forces and murdering hundreds of thousands of innocent civilians. Soon they had built an empire that included Korea, large parts of China, and other territories in the Far East.

A proud samurai poses for a photograph in 1867, the last year of shogunate rule.

KAMIKAZE PILOTS

Toward the end of World War II, Japan was desperate. Inch by inch Allied forces were capturing Japanese-held territories. Military leaders thought back to an earlier time of trouble. They recalled how a kamikaze, or "divine wind," had miraculously defeated thirteenth-century Mongol invaders.

Japanese pilots were offered the honor of serving their country as modern-day kamikaze. The young men were cleansed through Shinto ceremonies. Many dressed in white clothes and red headbands as a symbol of their purification.

As they climbed aboard planes packed with explosives, the pilots pledged to meet again at Yasukini, a famous Shinto shrine dedicated to the country's war dead. Then they took to the skies in search of Allied warships. Like a terrible storm of the gods, they crashed their exploding planes into the enemy ships.

Japan's kamikaze pilots were inspired by ancient samurai ideals of duty, self-sacrifice, and courage. But their sacrifice was a useless gesture. In World War II no "divine wind" could save Japan from defeat and ruin.

Opponents crushed by the Japanese army were amazed and dismayed by the fighting spirit of its soldiers. Inspired by age-old samurai traditions, these modern-day warriors fought to the death rather than accepting defeat or capture. At the same time they treated their prisoners with terrible cruelty, because they believed that people who allowed themselves to be captured must be weaklings and cowards.

In 1941 Japan launched a surprise attack on the U.S. Pacific naval base at Pearl Harbor in Hawaii. The United States was the greatest military threat to Japan's growing empire in the Pacific, and the Japanese hoped to remove that threat by wiping out the American navy. That attack brought the U.S. into the war on the side of Great Britain, the Soviet Union, and the other Allied nations. Japan entered World War II siding with the Axis powers, Germany and Italy.

The samurai spirit ran strong in the Japanese forces who fought in World War II—in soldiers who chose death over defeat, in sword-wielding officers who led desperate charges against machine guns, in suicide pilots who crashed their planes into enemy warships. But the Allied forces were just as determined. Following some early victories, Japan suffered a series of humiliating defeats. In 1945, after the United States dropped atomic bombs on the Japanese cities of Hiroshima and Nagasaki, Japan was finally defeated. Emperor Hirohito formally removed Japan's military leaders from power and announced the country's surrender.

Business Warriors

After World War II the Japanese people were horrified at the devastation and suffering their military leaders had caused. They adopted a new constitution, abolishing the military and setting up a new democratic government. Never again would the samurai spirit have a chance to prove its strength in battle. But the traditions of the samurai found a new and less deadly form of expression in the peacetime world. In less than fifty years Japan rose from ruin to become a leading manufacturing nation. Observers looking for the secret behind this economic success story often point to traditions rooted in the country's samurai past.

Two Japanese businessmen bow in greeting, just as their ancestors would have hundreds of years ago.

Japanese businesses traditionally were built on bonds of loyalty between employer and worker—a relationship often compared to the bond between a feudal lord and his followers. Employees often worked for the same company all their lives. Large companies might provide inexpensive housing, health care, and recreational facilities, and host after-work parties and weekend outings. Bosses took a warm interest in their employees' personal lives, offering advice and sometimes arranging dates or even marriages for single workers. In return for all this kindness and generosity, Japanese workers gave their companies loyalty and devoted service. Most employees of large companies worked six days a week. They often labored late into the night, without overtime pay, and gave up vacations and holidays to meet job responsibilities.

A number of Western business leaders studied and copied some of the traditional practices of Japanese companies. Some businesspeople even searched deep into the country's samurai past for the secret behind its business triumphs. One book written by a famous seventeenth-century samurai swordsman found a new audience among U.S. business leaders. *The Book of Five Rings* by Miyamoto Musashi offered advice on mental discipline and fighting techniques. American businesspeople turned Musashi's tips for attacking enemies into guidelines for outselling competing firms.

Modern times have brought some changes to Japan's traditional business practices. Beginning in the early 1990s the country's economy suffered a severe slowdown, or recession. Business production dropped, prices and wages fell, and thousands of workers lost their jobs. In these uncertain times many young people no longer feel quite the same loyalty to their employers as their parents and grandparents did. Young Japanese may change jobs or leave a company to start their own businesses. Some work fewer overtime hours so that they can spend time with their families. Like people around the world, they may even complain about having to work too hard.

Surviving Traditions

When Japanese workers grumble about their jobs, they do it at home or among close friends, not to the boss. The respect for authority that was a mark of Japanese society for hundreds of years is still very much alive

CHILDREN AND WOMEN IN MODERN JAPAN

The Japanese boy who obeys his parents and the Japanese girl who works hard at school are modern examples of old-time samurai ideals. From their earliest years Japanese children are taught the values of respect, education, and hard work. They go to school five and a half days a week, do five to six hours of homework a night, and may also attend special "cram schools" in the evenings and on weekends. All this studying prepares them for the difficult entrance exams given by the best elementary schools, high schools, and universities. Students work very hard to do well on these exams and bring honor to their schools and families.

Boys who graduate from a top university can look forward to jobs with Japan's leading companies. For girls, job opportunities are not as bright. The old samurai and Confucian traditions that placed women below men in social rank and importance have been slow to change. Though Japan's constitution gives women equal rights, many Japanese men still expect women to remain quiet and submissive. Today more Japanese women than ever before go to universities and work outside the home. But even well-educated women generally end up with lower-level, lower-paying jobs than men.

today. Many other customs and beliefs from the days of the samurai remain a part of everyday life in Japan.

Just as a warrior put the good of his clan above his own personal interests, the Japanese are loyal to their companies, schools, and families. One person's failure causes shame among the whole group. One member's success makes everyone feel proud. Strict rules of behavior ensure that all members of a group get along. Since ancient times these rules dictate the proper way to bow, eat, dress, play games, offer gifts, and do just about everything else.

Tradition also remains alive in Shinto shrines and Buddhist temples all across Japan. Though the Japanese no longer believe that their emperor is divine, they still practice ancient Shinto rituals and enjoy Shinto festivals. Many people ask a Shinto priest to marry them and bless their new home. Most Japanese also follow Buddhist teachings, pray at Buddhist temples, and are buried with Buddhist ceremonies. They may keep a small shrine at home in memory of relatives who have died, and they still welcome visiting ancestor spirits during the festival of Bon.

Traditional arts from the days of the samurai remain important. Most Japanese homes proudly display examples of their country's world-famous pottery, lacquerware, calligraphy, and painting. Japanese men and women still perform the tea ceremony for their families and special friends. Noh, Kabuki, and Bunraku plays are performed onstage and on television.

In Japan and around the world popular novels, movies, and television programs have been based on the days of the samurai. Though Japan today is a modern, democratic nation, its people are still fascinated by stories of their warrior traditions. Sometimes they take a humorous look at the past. One popular TV game show poked fun at the samurai's heroic endurance.

The graceful movements and splendid costumes of Noh drama live on in modern-day performances.

Japanese puppeteers entertain audiences with the traditional art of Bunraku, or puppet theater.

Teams of contestants on the program suffered through pies in the face, mud showers, and other "tortures," while home and studio audiences cheered the most courageous "warriors."

The Spirit in Martial Arts

One of the most important ways samurai traditions have been passed on to the outside world is through the martial arts. Today many forms of ancient Japanese fighting arts are practiced around the world for self-defense and the building of strength and character. Most popular are the arts of judo, karate, and kendo.

Judo, or "the way of gentleness," grew out of an ancient and deadly fighting art called jujitsu (joo-JIHT-soo). The first judo

SUMO WRESTLING

One of Japan's most popular sports is also its oldest. Sumo, or Japanese-style wrestling, began fifteen hundred years ago as a part of harvest rituals performed at Shinto shrines. In the days of the samurai, sumo became a popular spectator sport. Today millions of Japanese fans watch sumo tournaments in person and on television.

In a sumo match two huge, full-bellied wrestlers wearing loincloths fight inside a ring. Each tries to lift or push his opponent out of the ring or make him touch the ground inside the ring with some part of his body besides his feet. Sumo is a speedy sport, with most matches lasting only a few seconds.

Ancient customs and ceremonies are an important part of sumo. Strict rules dictate the way wrestlers enter the ring, bow, stomp their feet, circle about, and try to outstare their opponents. Following practices that have not changed in hundreds of years, sumo wrestlers sprinkle salt to purify the ring and clap their hands to get the gods' attention. There are about seventy different precisely defined methods of attacking an opponent in sumo. Just like samurai spectators hundreds of years ago, modern Japanese fans recognize and enthusiastically applaud each one.

Ancient ceremonies surround every action in a sumo wrestling match.

school opened in Japan after the Meiji Restoration, with the aim of preserving traditional fighting methods and samurai values. Today judo is an Olympic event in which contestants use skilled movements to throw their opponents. In judo schools worldwide, students train to develop strong bodies, mental discipline, and high moral values.

Karate-do, or "the way of the empty hand," is a method of fighting that uses kicks and punches instead of weapons. Developed by Buddhist priests in ancient China, karate was introduced to Japan at the beginning of the twentieth century. The ancient fighting art was combined with traditional samurai combat and training methods. Modern karate students learn techniques for self-defense and attack as well as a strictly defined series of movements called kata (KAH-tuh), or forms. The kata are designed to build self-confidence, determination, and total control of the emotions, body, and mind.

In samurai Japan warriors practiced their swordsmanship in schools of kendo, or "the way of the sword." Today Japanese students learn kendo in public and private schools, and the art is becoming increasingly popular in the West. Kendo competitors fence with bamboo swords, trying to score points by hitting targets on an opponent's armor. All the moves and thrusts are strictly detailed. Kendo aims to strengthen the body and spirit, building aggressiveness and courage.

Another martial art popular in Japan is *kyudo* (kee-yoo-doh), or "the way of the bow." A form of archery developed by Zen Buddhist monks, *kyudo* involves much more than shooting an arrow at a target. One Westerner who studied under a *kyudo* master described the art as "an ability whose origin is to be sought in spiritual exercises and whose aim consists of hitting a spiritual goal." To students of *kyudo*, the art of shooting the arrow is a form of meditation and religious enlightenment. The archer focusing on a target achieves peace and perfect harmony as the bow, arrow, and target merge into one.

Hundreds of thousands of people around the world have dedicated years to the study of *kyudo* and other Japanese martial arts. Their efforts have helped preserve and strengthen the best of the samurai ideals and traditions. Today a student bows respectfully in a martial arts class, a Japanese worker labors to build a better product, a family admires the cherry blossoms in a Japanese garden . . . and the samurai spirit lives on.

Samurai Japan: A Time Line

PREHISTORIC PERIOD	CLASSICAL PERIOD NARA PERIOD	HEIAN PERIOD
c. 8000 B.C.E.	400 C.E.	794

PREHISTORIC PERIOD
c. 8000 B.C.E.–400 C.E.

c. 8000 B.C.E.
Primitive Jomon
hunter-gatherer culture

c. 300 B.C.E.
Yayoi culture introduces
rice farming, displaces
Yomon

c. 300–600 C.E.
Kofun (tomb) stage of
Yayoi culture—leaders
buried in large
earthen tombs

CLASSICAL PERIOD
NARA PERIOD
400–794

c. 400
Yamato clan
gains dominance

c. 530
Introduction of Buddhism
to Japan

593
Soga clan's Prince Shotoku
becomes regent

645
Fujiwara clan gains
dominance; Taika
(Great Change)
Reforms redistribute land

710
First permanent
capital founded in Nara

784
Capital moved to Nagaoka

HEIAN PERIOD
794–1185

794
Capital moved to Heian (Kyoto)

c. 1000
The Tale of Genji written

1156
Hogen Incident—battle between
Taira and Minamoto/Fujiwara
forces

1160
Heiji Insurrection—
battle between Taira and
Minamoto; end of
Fujiwara power

1180–1185
Gempei War—
Minamoto defeat Taira

KAMAKURA SHOGUNATE	ASHIKAGA/ MUROMACHI SHOGUNATE	PERIOD OF UNIFICATION TOKUGAWA SHOGUNATE

1185   **1338**   **1573**   **1868**

KAMAKURA SHOGUNATE
1185–1338

1185
Military government
established at Kamakura

1192
Minamoto Yoritomo
becomes shogun

1199
Death of Yoritomo

1203
Hojo clan
gains dominance

1274 and **1281**
Mongol invasions

1333
Ashikaga displace Hojo

ASHIKAGA/
MUROMACHI SHOGUNATE
1338–1573

1336–1392
Civil war between
Northern and Southern
courts

1338
Ashikaga shogunate
established

1392
Northern and Southern
courts reunited

1467–1477
Onin War

1467–1568
Age of the Country at War

1509
Daisen-in garden built
in Kyoto

1542 or **1543**
First Europeans arrive

1549
Frances Xavier leads
Jesuit missionaries
to Japan

1568
Oda Nobunaga takes
control of Kyoto

PERIOD OF UNIFICATION
TOKUGAWA SHOGUNATE
1573–1868

1582
Death of Nobunaga

1590
Toyotomi Hideyoshi
completes unification of Japan

1592 and **1597**
Hideyoshi invades Korea

1598
Death of Hideyoshi

1603
Tokugawa Ieyasu
becomes shogun

1612
Ieyasu issues order
banning Christianity

1638
National seclusion order
restricts foreign trade

1854
Treaty of Kanagawa opens
Japanese ports

1868
Shogunate rule abolished;
Meiji Restoration returns
emperor to power

GLOSSARY

ashigaru (ahsh-ee-gah-roo)**:** lower-class foot soldiers who served in a samurai army; in English, "light feet"

Buddhism (BOO-diz-um)**:** the religion based on the fifth-century B.C.E. teachings of the Indian wise man known as the Buddha, or "Enlightened One," emphasizing rules of ideal behavior and the practice of meditation

Bunraku (bun-RAH-koo)**:** a popular form of Japanese theater in which all the roles are played by large wooden puppets

Bushido (BU-shee-doh)**:** the code of honorable conduct practiced by the samurai; in English, "the way of the warrior"

calligraphy: the art of beautiful handwriting

clan: a large group of people who are descended from the same ancestor

Confucianism: the philosophy based on the fifth-century B.C.E. teachings of the Chinese wise man known as Confucius, emphasizing duty, proper behavior, and fulfilling one's role in society

daimyo (DIE-mee-oh)**:** a powerful Japanese landowner who maintained a samurai army and a large estate; in English, "great name"

enlightenment: in Buddhism, the state of total knowledge and freedom from desire

feudal system: a political system in which a lord provides land and protection to his vassals, who in return give loyalty and service

haiku (HIE-koo)**:** an unrhymed Japanese poem with three lines containing five, seven, and five syllables

*hakama***:** a pair of wide trousers with slitted slides, worn by samurai men

hara-kiri (hair-ih-KIR-ee)**:** the slang term for seppuku

ikebana (ih-kay-BAH-nuh)**:** the art of flower arranging

imperial: relating to an emperor, empress, or empire

judo: martial art based on the samurai fighting method jujitsu, using skilled movements to throw or trap an opponent; in English, "the way of gentleness"

Kabuki (kuh-BOO-kee): a popular form of Japanese theater, with singing and dancing performed in an exaggerated manner

kami (KAH-mee): the spirits considered sacred in the Shinto religion; can also mean holiness or sacredness

kamikaze (kah-mih-KAH-zee): the storms that destroyed the Mongol fleet in 1281; in English, "divine wind." The name also was adopted by Japanese suicide pilots during World War II.

kana (KAH-nuh): a Japanese system of writing that uses simplified characters; each kana character stands for a sound

kanji (KAHN-jee): a Japanese system of writing that uses characters borrowed from written Chinese; each kanji character stands for a word

karate-do: martial art based on traditional samurai fighting techniques, mostly using punches and kicks; in English, "the way of the empty hand"

kendo: martial art in which contestants fence with bamboo swords, using samurai fighting techniques; in English, "the way of the sword"

kyudo (kee-yoo-doh): a form of archery developed by Zen Buddhist monks; in English, "the way of the bow"

lacquerware: a decorative item made of wood or paper coated with lacquer, which is a varnish that hardens into a smooth, shiny surface

ninja: samurai who were specially trained to serve as spies and assassins

nirvana: in Buddhism, the state of enlightenment that releases a person's spirit from the cycle of reincarnation

Noh: a form of Japanese theater, traditionally favored by the upper classes, usually based on ancient legends

recession: a period in which a country's economy slows down and unemployment rises

regalia: the emblems or symbols of a royal family; the regalia of Japan's imperial family include a mirror, a sword, and jewels

regent: in Japan, someone who held the real power in the country by serving as chief adviser to the emperor

reincarnation: in Buddhism, rebirth of a person's spirit into a new body after death

renga: a form of Japanese poetry in which pairs of poets take turns making up the lines of a tanka; in English, "linked verse"

ritual: a series of special ceremonies repeatedly performed in a certain fixed way

samurai (SA-muh-rye): the warrior class of Japan from the tenth to mid–nineteenth centuries; in English, "those who serve"

sect: group or division

seppuku (seh-POO-koo): a ritual suicide performed by a samurai to regain lost honor

Shinto: the ancient religion of Japan, based on reverence for a host of gods and goddesses, nature spirits, and ancestor spirits; in English, "the way of the gods"

shogun: one of the military rulers of Japan from the twelfth to mid–nineteenth centuries

shogunate: the military government headed by the shogun

sumi-e (SOO-mee-eh): a painting style that uses black ink applied with a brush

tanka: an unrhymed Japanese poem with five lines containing five, seven, five, seven, and seven syllables

tatami (tah-TAH-mee): a straw mat used as a floor covering in a Japanese home

torii (TOHR-ee-ee): the sacred gateway of a Shinto shrine

vassal: a person under the protection of a feudal lord, to whom he or she has sworn to give loyalty and service

FOR FURTHER READING

Blumberg, Rhoda. *Commodore Perry in the Land of the Shogun.* New York: Lothrop, Lee & Shepard, 1985.

Galvin, Irene Flum. *Japan: A Modern Land with Ancient Roots.* Tarrytown, NY: Marshall Cavendish, 1996.

Hall, Eleanor J. *Life among the Samurai.* San Diego: Lucent Books, 1999.

Kimmel, Eric A. *Sword of the Samurai: Adventure Stories from Japan.* San Diego: Harcourt Brace, 1999.

MacDonald, Fiona. *A Samurai Castle.* New York: Peter Bedrick Books, 1995.

Nardo, Don. *Traditional Japan.* San Diego: Lucent Books, 1995.

Odijk, Pamela. *The Japanese.* Englewood Cliffs, NJ: Silver Burdett, 1989.

Roberts, Jenny. *Samurai Warriors.* New York: Gloucester Press, 1990.

Turnbull, Stephen R. *Warlords of Japan.* London: Sampson Low, 1979.

ON-LINE INFORMATION*

Hooker, Richard. *Feudal Japan.*
[*http://www.wsu.edu/~dee/FEUJAPAN/CONTENTS.HTM*].

Lindemans, M.F. *Encyclopedia Mythica.*
[*http://www.pantheon.org/mythica/areas/japanese*].

The Virtual Museum of Traditional Japanese Arts.
[*http://jin.jcic.or.jp/museum/index.html*].

*Websites change from time to time. For additional on-line information, check with the media specialist at your local library.

BIBLIOGRAPHY

Blumberg, Rhoda. *Commodore Perry in the Land of the Shogun.* New York: Lothrop, Lee & Shepard, 1985.

Bottomley, Ian, and Anthony P. Hopson. *Arms and Armor of the Samurai.* Greenwich, CT: Brompton Books, 1988.

Cook, Harry. *Samurai: The Story of a Warrior Tradition.* New York: Sterling Publishing, 1993.

DeMente, Boye Lafayette. *Japan's Secret Weapon: The Kata Factor.* Phoenix: Phoenix Books, 1990.

Galvin, Irene Flum. *Japan: A Modern Land with Ancient Roots.* Tarrytown, NY: Marshall Cavendish, 1996.

Gibson, Michael. *The Samurai of Japan.* London: Wayland Publishers, 1973.

Greene, Carol. *Japan.* Chicago: Childrens Press, 1983.

Japan: An Illustrated Encyclopedia. Tokyo: Kodansha Ltd., 1993.

Keene, Donald, ed. *Anthology of Japanese Literature.* New York: Grove Press, 1955.

Langone, John. *In the Shogun's Shadow: Understanding a Changing Japan.* Boston: Little, Brown, 1994.

Lewis, Brenda Ralph. *Growing Up in Samurai Japan.* London: Batsford Academic and Educational Limited, 1981.

MacDonald, Fiona, David Antram, and John James. *A Samurai Castle.* New York: Peter Bedrick Books, 1995.

Nardo, Don. *Traditional Japan.* San Diego: Lucent Books, 1995.

———. *Modern Japan.* San Diego: Lucent Books, 1995.

Odijk, Pamela. *The Japanese.* Englewood Cliffs, NJ: Silver Burdett, 1989.

Reischauer, Edwin O. *The Japanese.* Cambridge, MA: Harvard University Press, Belknap Press, 1977.

Roberts, Jenny. *Samurai Warriors.* New York: Gloucester Press, 1990.

Sato, Hiroaki. *Legends of the Samurai*. Woodstock, NY: Overlook Press, 1995.

Sparling, Kathryn, trans. *The Way of the Samurai: Yukio Mishima on* Hagakure *in Modern Life*. New York: Basic Books, 1977.

Steel, Anne. *How They Lived: A Samurai Warrior*. Vero Beach, FL: Rourke Enterprises, 1988.

Turnbull, Stephen R. *The Book of the Samurai: The Warrior Class of Japan*. New York: Arco Publishing, 1982.

———. *Samurai Warlords: The Book of the Daimyo*. London: Blandford Press, 1989.

———. *Warlords of Japan*. London: Sampson Low, 1979.

Varley, H. Paul, with Ivan Morris and Nobuko Morris. *Samurai*. New York: Delacorte Press, 1970.

INDEX

Page numbers for illustrations are in boldface

ABOUT THE AUTHOR

Virginia Schomp has written dozens of books for young readers, including another title in the CULTURES OF THE PAST series, *The Ancient Greeks*. She lives in Monticello, New York, with her husband, Richard, and their son, Chip. When she's not busy writing, Ms. Schomp loves to spend time outdoors, working in her gardens. Since she began studying the culture and arts of ancient Japan, she has stopped fighting the boulders and pebbles that crop up everywhere in the Catskill Mountains region and has started work on a (soon-to-be-beautiful) Japanese-style rock garden.